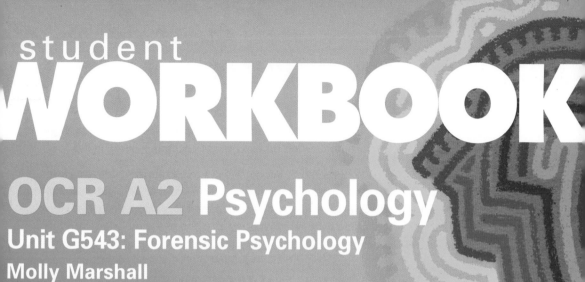

student WORKBOOK

OCR A2 Psychology
Unit G543: Forensic Psychology
Molly Marshall

D1351081

Philip Allan Updates, an imprint of Hodder Education, an Hachette UK company, Market Place, Deddington, Oxfordshire OX15 0SE

Orders
Bookpoint Ltd, 130 Milton Park, Abingdon, Oxfordshire OX14 4SB
tel: 01235 827720   fax: 01235 400454
e-mail: uk.orders@bookpoint.co.uk

Lines are open 9.00 a.m.–5.00 p.m., Monday to Saturday, with a 24-hour message answering service. You can also order through the Philip Allan Updates website: www.philipallan.co.uk

ISBN 978-1-4441-0848-4
© Philip Allan Updates 2010
First printed 2010
Impression number 5 4 3 2 1
Year 2013 2012 2011 2010

Printed in Spain

Environmental information
Hachette UK's policy is to use papers that are natural, renewable and recyclable products and made from wood grown in sustainable forests. The logging and manufacturing processes are expected to conform to the environmental regulations of the country of origin.

Introduction

This workbook is designed to support your study of OCR A2 Unit G543: Forensic Psychology. The aim is to help you to increase your understanding of forensic psychology and to improve your skills in answering the types of question that you might encounter in the exam.

The workbook includes a variety of research, but not always the 'example study' suggested in the OCR specification. If you need more information on any of the research, you could access the OCR website: **www.ocr.org.uk**. The questions are designed to support you as you develop skills of analysis, interpretation and evaluation. Writing answers to the questions will help you learn to communicate your knowledge and understanding of psychology in a clear and effective manner. As you complete the workbook, you should become confident that you are learning the content required for the exam and how to write answers that will achieve high marks.

The OCR specification requires you to be able to describe and evaluate psychological research in four topics in forensic psychology:
- turning to crime
- making a case
- reaching a verdict
- after a guilty verdict

The workbook is organised into four topics:
- Topic 1 focuses on psychological research into why people turn to crime.
- Topic 2 looks at how psychology can inform the investigative process — making a case.
- Topic 3 examines psychological research into behaviour in the courtroom — reaching a verdict.
- Topic 4 focuses on psychological research into imprisonment, alternatives to imprisonment and offender treatment programmes — after a guilty verdict.

For each of these topics, you must be able to:
- discuss and apply psychological research methods, perspectives and issues
- actively seek to apply theory and evidence to the improvement of real-life events
- explore social, moral, cultural and spiritual issues where applicable
- consider how the core areas of psychology (cognitive, developmental, physiological, social and individual differences) studied at AS can inform our understanding of forensic psychology

To gain maximum benefit, you should complete the questions on each topic in the order given, as they become progressively more difficult. There are several ways in which you can use this workbook:
- As an integral part of your learning experience to be used in conjunction with your class notes, handouts and textbook. Periodically, your teacher might ask you to hand in your book for assessment.
- As a revision tool, in which case you should work through the topics, writing the answers as practice for the exam.
- As a combination of both. If, as you progress through the unit, you write answers to all the questions in this book, at the end of the course you will have created a valuable resource from which to revise.

Topic 1   Turning to crime

This topic focuses on explanations for criminal behaviour. It looks at psychological research into factors and influences that may explain why people turn to crime.
The three sections in this topic are:
- upbringing
- cognition
- biology

At the end of this topic, you should be able to:
- describe and evaluate psychological research into the reasons why people turn to crime
- discuss and apply psychological research methods, perspectives and issues when considering why people turn to crime

Item 1   Upbringing

Some psychological research suggests a nurture approach to why people turn to crime and looks at factors involved in upbringing.

D. P. Farrington, G. C. Barnes and S. Lambert (1996): offending in families

Aim: To test the hypothesis that problem families produce problem children. This research is part of a longitudinal study, the Cambridge Study in Delinquent Development, which followed one group of males from the age of 8 to 32 in interviews and from the age of 10 to 40 via their criminal records. This study looks at the association between the convictions of these males and the convictions of their biological parents and siblings.

Sample: The sample was 411 boys from inner-city areas of London, mostly born in 1953. Participants were selected by taking all 8- and 9-year-old boys from the registers of six state primary schools in one location in London. The boys were predominantly white and from working-class families. As a control, because there were 14 pairs of brothers in the original sample, 397 different families were involved in the research, and to avoid counting the same family more than once, one of each pair (the younger brother or a randomly selected twin) was excluded from this analysis.

Method: The Cambridge Study involved interviews with the children, and with their parents, and questionnaires were completed by teachers. Searches were carried out in the central Criminal Record Office in London to locate evidence of convictions of the males, their biological fathers and mothers, and their full brothers and sisters. Most commonly the offences were theft, burglary and unauthorised taking of motor vehicles, although they also included violence, vandalism, fraud and drug abuse.

Results: The Cambridge Study confirms the hypothesis that criminals are likely to have criminal relatives. When the participants were age 20, 48% of those with convicted fathers also had convictions, compared with 19% of those without convicted fathers; 54% of those with convicted mothers also had convictions, compared with 23% of those with non-convicted mothers. This link remained even when males with both mother and father with convictions were removed from the analysis. These results are confirmed when the participants were aged 40: 64% of the families contained one convicted person or more, and just 6% (23 families) of the families accounted for over half of all the convictions. Conviction of one family member is strongly associated with conviction of another family member, and about 75% of convicted parents had a convicted child; having a sibling who had been convicted (especially an older sibling) was also a strong predictor of conviction. **Conclusion:** Overall, the results suggest that offending is concentrated in families and tends to be transmitted from one generation to the next. However, as the authors point out, these results do not establish whether this is due to the influence of nature or nurture.

'The concentration of offending in families', *Legal and Criminological Psychology* 1, pp. 47–63

Item 2   Learning from others

Edwin Sutherland's differential association theory proposes that individuals learn the values, attitudes, techniques and motives for criminal behaviour through social interaction with others. The principles of Sutherland's theory can be summarised into key points:

- Criminal behaviour is learned through interaction with other persons in a process of communication.
- The principal part of the learning of criminal behaviour occurs within intimate personal groups, for example within criminal gangs.
- The learning of criminal behaviour includes techniques of committing the crime, as well as the motives, drives, rationalisations and attitudes.
- A person becomes delinquent because he or she adopts the norms and values of the criminal group in preference to the norms and values of non-criminal groups.
- Differential associations may vary in frequency, duration, priority and intensity.
- The process of learning criminal behaviour by association with criminal groups involves all of the mechanisms that are involved in any other learning.

Item 3   The social context of pathways to crime: PADS

The Peterborough Adolescent Development Study (PADS) represents the first phase (2002–07) of an ongoing ESRC-funded longitudinal study, the Peterborough Adolescent and Young Adult Development Study. For detailed information see: **www.scopic.ac.uk/StudiesPADS.html**.

Objectives

The main objective of PADS is to study the interaction between individual and environmental factors that lead to crime. It is designed to test the following hypotheses:

- Social mechanisms that influence age-related offending will vary with community context.
- Differences in individuals' routines, processes of decision-making, and perception of alternatives will play a significant role in accounting for that variation.

Specifically, it will investigate the causal role in offending of the following:

- moral values and the ability to exercise self-control (individual characteristics)
- temptations, provocations and deterrence (environmental characteristics)
- interaction through two situational mechanisms: the perception of alternatives and the process of choice

PADS is particularly interested in exploring and explaining how the changing social environment during adolescence and the period of transition into young adulthood influences the development of different young people's crime involvement.

Methodologies

Data were collected through:

- the Peterborough Community Survey (PCS)
- a retrospective questionnaire for parents (administered in a single one-to-one interview in 2003), which covered topics such as family life, childhood events, peer relationships and school experience
- psychometric tests (conducted during one-to-one interviews with participants), which assessed various cognitive capacities including memory, emotion, reasoning, moral reasoning, information processing, multi-tasking and concentration
- an annual or bi-annual young persons' questionnaire, which covered topics such as the young person's family life, school experience, peer relations, moral values and emotions, generalised self-control, perception of risk and consequences, temptations, offending and use of drugs and alcohol

The young persons' questionnaire was administered in small groups. Participants were led through each section of the questionnaire by a trained researcher who provided definitions and instructions, answered questions and ensured questionnaires were fully and accurately completed. This reduced non-response, increased reliability by immediately resolving participants' queries, and increased validity by ensuring participants understood key concepts, and consequently answered related questions, as intended.

Data on environments (including information on socio-demographics and neighbourhood characteristics) were also collected through:

- one-to-one interviews with parents
- interviewer-led, small-group questionnaires with young people
- the Peterborough Community Survey (PCS)

The PCS collected detailed data on small, geographically identifiable areas of Peterborough, including environmental and social/environmental data. Techniques were used to ensure an even distribution of responses, even from disadvantaged neighbourhoods.

Individual exposure to different environments was measured during one-to-one interviews with young people, during which data were gathered on participants' hourly activities over 4 days during the week prior to the interview: the last Friday and Saturday and two other most recent school days. For each hour, participants provided data on the setting (for example home, school, shopping centre), their companions (for example peers, parents, siblings) and their main activity (for example socialising, studying, playing football). Their geographical location was then identified using geo-coded maps. For each hour, participants were also asked if they were involved in risky situations, were victimised, committed an offence, used drugs or alcohol, or carried a weapon.

Findings (2007)

Key findings suggested the importance of the interaction between individual characteristics, especially moral values, and environmental factors such as monitoring and supervision, as well as the importance of separating causes of crime (such as poor moral values) from more distant 'causes of the causes' (such as disadvantage).

Individual variables — morality and self-control

Weak morality and low self-control both predicted participants' offending. There was an interaction between morality and self-control, such that low self-control was only related to offending for participants who also had weak morality.

The social environment

Participants' exposure to criminogenic environments (for example those with weak social cohesion and poor informal social control) was also related to their offending. Neighbourhood disadvantage is linked to the presence of criminogenic environments. However, PADS researchers found that it is not living in a disadvantaged area that leads to offending, but rather exposure to criminogenic environments (within and outside of one's neighbourhood). Thus it is the time spent in disadvantaged environments that is important to offending, and not necessarily the fact that one's area of residence is disadvantaged.

Developmental effects

Family variables (such as family structure, family climate and family social position) and school variables (for example school bonds) were significantly related to levels of morality and self-control; participants who experienced greater parental care/nurturing, regardless of family structure or social position, and stronger school bonds, exhibited greater levels of morality and self-control. In fact, morality and self-control mediated the relationship between family and school variables and offending, suggesting that family and school variables influence offending only through their role in determining young people's levels of morality and self-control.

Individual environment interactions

The data suggest that exposure to criminogenic contexts (environmental factors) leads to offending specifically for participants with weaker morality and lower self-control (i.e. greater individual propensity). This suggests that participants with greater individual propensity may be more susceptible to environmental inducements to offend. This has implications for intervention practices. PADS researchers have also found that deterrence is only effective for participants who consider committing an offence. Fear of the consequences of offending was only important in explaining the offending (or non-offending) of participants who reported being regularly tempted to offend.

Implications

The study has the potential to inform policy and practice because it provides a unique perspective on young people, their offending behaviour and the environments in which those behaviours occur. This will advance understanding of the direct causes of crime, as well as the causes of the causes, which can provide a clearer foundation for developing prevention and intervention strategies.

Professor Per-Olof Wikström, 'Individual risk, lifestyle risk and adolescent offending', University of Cambridge

Item 4   Cognition and rationality

Do criminals think rationally?

Yochelson and Samenow (1976) focused on the idea that criminals make rational choices by using their cognitive processes but they emphasise the role of cognitive dysfunction — suggesting that criminals have distinct and faulty 'thinking patterns'. They interviewed 240 male offenders who had been referred to their hospital for 'determination of competency' and concluded that the criminals were less intelligent than non-criminals but did have free choice. They interviewed a small number of offenders who were hardcore criminals. They identified 40 'errors', which fall into three categories:

- criminal thinking patterns, characterised by a simultaneous fear and need for power and control
- automatic thinking errors, including a lack of empathy and failure to accept obligations and a secretive communication style
- crime-related thinking errors, including optimistic fantasising about criminal acts with no regard to deterrent factors

This suggests that criminals planned and thought about their actions and that this kind of irrational thinking needs to be tackled when treating or punishing them.

Mandracchia et al. (2007): criminal thinking patterns

Aim: To identify the defining characteristics of criminal thinking.

Method: Psychometric tests (self-report) and factor analysis.

Participants: Opportunity sample (selected by prison officers) — 435 prisoners in six prisons in Texas, average age 36, age range 18–76:

- 47% single, 24% married, 25% divorced/separated
- 64% black American or Hispanic
- 51% minimum secure, 18% medium secure, 19% maximum secure

Types of crime

- 20% burglary/robbery
- 17% drug crimes
- 9% assault/battery
- 8% sex crime

Sentences ranged from 6 months to 100 years; the average sentence was 20 years and the average time served was 5.5 years. The participants were a representative sample of prisoners in Texas state prisons. All gave informed consent and were assured of confidentiality.

Procedures: Participants completed psychometric tests in groups — the test was the Measure of Offender Thinking Styles (MOTS), which measures 77 thinking styles. There are three items (questions) per each thinking style, in all 231 questions, and the result is analysed by factor analysis.

Findings: Criminal thinking is defined by three thinking styles:

- control (the need for power and control)
- cognitive immaturity (for example self-pity and over-generalisation)
- egocentricity (focusing on self and own needs and wants)

Conclusions: Criminals do think differently to non-criminals, and the way criminals think can be assessed. Criminal thinking allows self-indulgent and rash behaviour that is contrary to accepted social standards and is irrational, unorganised, subjective and leads to immediate gratification. Criminals can be treated to help them change the way they think, and treatment should be offered to first offenders.

'Inmate thinking patterns: an empirical investigation', *Criminal Justice and Behavior* **34**, pp. 1029–43

Item 5 Cognition and morality

Kohlberg's stages of moral development

Kohlberg developed a theory of moral development based closely on Piaget's stages of cognitive development. These three levels are defined as pre-conventional, conventional and post-conventional morality, and each level consists of two separate stages.

Level 1: pre-conventional morality

Stages 1 and 2 compose the lowest level of moral reasoning, in which the focus is on rules and the consequences of breaking them.

- During stage 1, goodness (or badness) is determined by consequences, so that an act is not bad if one can get away with it.
- At stage 2, children conform to rules in order to gain rewards, and they will do nice things for other people if they think they will benefit from it in the long run.

Level 2: conventional morality (conformity)

Stages 3 and 4 correspond to the age of Piaget's concrete operations. An increased understanding of others' intentions, a decrease in egocentrism, and the desire to win praise from others marks this level.

- Stage 3 is often called the 'good girl/good boy' stage, when children obey rules to gain praise and live up to social roles and expectations.
- Stage 4 concerns the importance of obeying rules and respecting authority because of their roles in maintaining a functioning society.

Level 3: post-conventional morality (autonomous)

This last level of moral reasoning is marked by an internal commitment to an individual's set of values.

- In stage 5, moral actions are those that express the will of the majority (democracy) but also maximise social welfare.
- Stage 6 is called universal ethical principles and is marked by a set of self-defined ethical principles that determine right and wrong based on ideas of universal justice and respect for human rights and dignity.

Determining levels of morality

To determine a child's level of morality, Kohlberg paid attention to the reasoning behind the answer rather than the answer itself. For example, having heard the Heinz dilemma, a child might respond that something is wrong because it breaks the law, but it is important to know whether he or she thinks laws should be upheld because otherwise one will be punished, or because laws are needed to maintain social order.

Are criminals less moral than non-criminals?

In a natural experiment, Palmer and Hilling (1998) compared moral reasoning between delinquents and non-delinquents. The sample consisted of 126 convicted male and female offenders in a young offenders' institution, and 22 male and 210 female non-offenders. All were from the English Midlands and aged 13–22 years old. All participants were given Socio-Moral Reflection Measure Short Form (SRM-SF), which contains 11 questions based on moral dilemmas (for example not taking things that belong to others and keeping a promise to a friend). The delinquent group showed less mature moral reasoning. In the male groups, there was a difference on 10 out of 11 questions, and in the female group it was 7 out of 11.

Item 6 Biological explanations

A. Raine and J. H. Liu (1998): biological risk factors and crime

Aim: To identify biological risk factors for violence and crime.

Study 1: Research question: are low levels of physiological arousal a predictor of offending behaviour?

Sample: The sample consisted of 101 15-year-old boys.

Method: This is a correlation study, which looked for a relationship between a number of physiological measures (skin conductance, EEG and heart rate) taken at age 15 and the numbers of offences that they had committed by the age of 24.

Results: The authors report a strong correlation between the two measures. Those committing crimes had significantly lower heart rates, reduced skin conductance and more slow-wave EEG theta activity than non-criminals. The authors claim that these measures correctly classified 74.7% of all participants as criminal or non-criminal.

'Biological predispositions to violence and their implications for biosocial treatment and prevention', *Psychology, Crime and Law* **4**, pp. 107–25

Item 7 Biological and socio-cognitive interaction

S. Bennett, P. Farrington and L. R. Huesmann (2004)

Research shows higher rates of offending, especially violent offending, for males than for females. Research suggests that gender differences in the development of social cognition may help to explain gender differences in crime and violence. How an individual responds to a stressful event or risk factor depends on how the person perceives the event. Social information-processing skills allow individuals to encode information, interpret and consider the risks and benefits of a particular action, and determine an appropriate response based on their repertoire of behavioural scripts. Certain ways of processing social information may help to protect the individual from personal, social, environmental or situational pressures towards criminal behaviour.

One of the reasons females have lower rates of offending is because they develop social-cognitive skills earlier in life than males and because they have better pro-social skills. The superior social-cognitive skills of females are influenced by many factors, including better interhemispheric communication, fewer frontal lobe deficits, greater verbal ability, and differential socialisation by parents and peers.

Institute of Criminology, Cambridge University, UK, and Institute for Social Research, University of Michigan, USA

Questions

1 Read Item 1.

a Outline research suggesting that upbringing influences people to turn to crime.

b Using the issues of ecological validity and generalisability, evaluate the research you have outlined.

c Assess the usefulness of the research you have outlined.

2 Read Items 2 and 3.

a Outline research suggesting that the social environment influences people to turn to crime.

b Assess *one* methodological strength and *one* limitation of the research outlined.

c Assess the usefulness of the research you outlined in Question 2a.

3 Read Items 4 and 5.

   a Outline research suggesting that cognitive factors (criminal thinking patterns) explain why people commit crimes.

b Evaluate the research you outlined.

c Assess the usefulness of the research you outlined.

4 Read Items 6 and 7.

a Outline research suggesting that biological factors explain why people to turn to crime.

b Assess *one* strength and *one* limitation of the research you outlined.

c Discuss *two* problems faced by psychologists who research biological explanations for criminal behaviour.

....

....

....

....

....

....

....

....

d Discuss, using evidence, why biological explanations for criminal behaviour may be described as reductionist.

....

....

....

....

....

....

....

....

....

....

....

....

....

....

....

5 Exam practice

Read Items 1–7. Make a plan for this essay, write it out in full and hand it in to be assessed.

a Describe *two* explanations as to why people turn to crime.

b How useful are psychological explanations of criminal behaviour? In terms of reductionism, evaluate explanations of why people turn to crime.

Topic 2   Making a case

The three sections in this topic are:
- interviewing witnesses
- interviewing suspects
- creating a profile

At the end of this topic, you should be able to:
- describe and evaluate psychological research into aspects of the investigative process
- discuss and apply psychological research methods, perspectives and issues when considering aspects of the investigative process

Item 1   Interviewing witnesses: the cognitive interview

Traditionally, police officers and lawyers use the standard interview procedure, which involves a period of free recall about the event followed by specific questions on the information revealed.

Geiselman et al. (1986) suggested that using the cognitive interview instead would result in a 30% improvement in recall, with no increase in the number of incorrect responses. This type of interview elicits almost twice as much information but with no loss of accuracy. It involves:
- mentally reinstating the context of the event, i.e. the sounds, smells, feelings experienced during the event
- asking witnesses to recall the event in various orders, or in reverse order
- asking witnesses to report absolutely everything, regardless of the perceived importance of the information
- recalling the event from a variety of perspectives, for example imagining what the scene must have looked like from the point of view of several characters there at the time

Each of these retrieval mnemonics allows the witness to review the event without the interference of leading questions but forces him or her to scrutinise his or her memory record. The technique aims to maximise the number of potential retrieval routes and to benefit from overlaps, hopefully triggering otherwise forgotten details of the event.

> **R. P. Fisher, R. E. Geiselman and M. Amador (1989): field testing the cognitive interview**
> **Aim:** To compare the performance of experienced detectives pre- and post-training in cognitive interviewing techniques and to compare their performance post-training with a control group.
> **Participants:** Sixteen experienced detectives in Florida; seven completed the cognitive interviewing course, and their performance was compared with nine untrained controls.
> **Method:** All 16 detectives tape-recorded several interviews. Each detective recorded between five and seven interviews over a period of 4 months, and a total of 88 interviews

were recorded. These were mainly with victims of commercial robbery or purse snatching. At the end of this stage, the two groups were created. Seven detectives underwent four 1-hour sessions of training. After training, these seven detectives, and six of the remaining nine, recorded between two and seven interviews. A total of 47 interviews were recorded over 7 months. Interviews were transcribed and scored by independent judges, and the number of relevant, factual and objective statements were recorded.

Findings: Forty-seven percent more information was recorded in the post-training interviews than in the pre-training interviews. Six of the seven detectives in this group did better post-training with only one doing worse — the authors note that this detective was not using the suggestions given during training.

Sixty-three percent more information was recorded in the interviews conducted by the trained detectives compared with the control group.

Conclusion: These results clearly show the effectiveness of the cognitive interviewing technique over traditional interviewing methods; it could also be suggested that this training is relatively easy to provide.

'Field test of the cognitive interview: enhancing the recollection of actual victims and witnesses of crime', *Journal of Applied Psychology* **74** (5), pp. 722–27

Item 2   Interviewing witnesses: question order

V. Morris and P. E. Morris (1985): question order and eyewitness recall

Aim: To investigate whether asking participants questions that follow the order of events will lead to better recall.

Sample: Ninety-six people aged 18–44. This was an opportunity sample of friends and neighbours of the authors. Participants were volunteers and were not paid for participating.

Method: This is an experiment with independent measures. Two groups of 48 participants were shown one of two short films, each of which culminated in a chase scene. Two films were used to ensure that effects would generalise beyond a single film sequence. One was a clip of *Starsky and Hutch* and the other was of unfamiliar people. Both clips were approximately 5 minutes long, they involved two central characters being pursued and culminated in a chase sequence and the main event. Participants were tested at home or in the experimenter's home, either individually or in small groups, and before being questioned were asked to write a free narrative account of the film. The participants were allocated to one of four 'questioning' conditions:

- Random order — question order randomised by use of a random number table
- Time sequence — questions asked in order
- Central character — questions about the central character first, followed by questions about the event in time sequence
- Main event — all questions about the chase asked first, rest following time sequence

Twenty-five questions were asked on each film. Questions covered a range of detail, from what was said by major and minor characters, to their appearance and behaviour and other details about the scene.

Findings: Free narrative accounts were scored by giving one mark for each correct detail. Less than one incorrect detail per person was recorded. Mean scores were 30.8 (Film A) and 28.6 (Film B). Results from the questions showed that time sequence led to the best recall.

Question order				
	Time sequence	**Central character**	**Main event**	**Random**
% correct	69	66	60	58

This suggests that if witnesses are asked questions in the time sequence of the event, they may recall more information.

'The influence of question order on eyewitness accuracy', *British Journal of Psychology* **76**, pp. 365–71

Item 3 Interviewing witnesses: face recognition

Eyewitness identification of faces may not be reliable, as is indicated by the following two studies.

Ainsworth (1995) showed participants a news story about sex assaults, which included a photofit of a suspect and a photo of a 'good Samaritan' who had helped one of the victims. One week later, the same participants were asked to identify the suspect from selection of six photos. In one condition, the photos included the suspect, but in another condition, the photos included the 'Samaritan' but not the suspect.

In the 'suspect included' condition, 40% of the participants correctly picked the suspect, but in the 'suspect not included' condition, 50% of the participants incorrectly picked the 'good Samaritan'.

Shepherd, Davies and Ellis (1978) asked participants to view a face for 30 seconds and then asked them to construct a photofit. The description of the 'face' differed — half the participants were told the face was of a 'brave captain of a lifeboat', but half were told the face was of a 'mass murderer'. The photofit pictures produced of the 'mass murderer' were judged to be more cruel, unpleasant and unintelligent by independent judges.

Bruce et al. (1988): facial recognition
Aim: To investigate the relative recognisability of internal features (eyes, brows, nose and mouth) and external features (head shape, hair and ears) in facial recognition.
Procedure: In experiment 1, the participants were given pictures of 10 celebrities and asked to match the correct composite image to the celebrity from the 40 composites given. Group 1 was given complete composites, group 2 composites containing only internal features (eyes,

nose, mouth) and group 3 external feature (head shape, hair and ears) composites. Each face was clean-shaven and spectacles were avoided.

Experiment 2 used a photo array, and the task was to identify the celebrity composites from the array. The task was made either easy (very different from target face) or hard (very similar to target face). Once again, the composites were composed of either external or internal features.

Findings: In experiment 1, 42% of whole composites and those of external features were sorted correctly, compared with only 19.5% of internal features.

In experiment 2, external features were identified 42% of the time, compared with just 24% of internal features.

Conclusion: Participants performed equally well with both whole composites and external features. This shows that external features are more important for facial recognition and that faces are processed holistically. This has implications for facial reconstructions that involve witnesses picking internal features from a book.

D. F. Christie and H. D. Ellis (1981): verbal recall of faces and police photofits

Aim: To compare the effectiveness of verbal recall of faces with that of the photofit technique used by the police.

Sample: The sample of 36 participants recruited from the psychology department subject panel included 27 women and nine men, aged between 29 and 63 years.

Method: The experiment was conducted in two stages:
- face recall by description and by photofit construction
- evaluation (by 'judges') of their respective accuracy

Procedures: Participants were shown target faces (six different faces) and then, from memory, gave a verbal description and constructed a photofit likeness.

All participants were tested individually and were shown the target face for 60 seconds. They were then asked to describe the face and all the details were recorded. At the end of the description, if the participant had not mentioned any of the five photofit features, they were prompted to do so. The subject then constructed a visual likeness using the photofit kit. The final likeness was photographed for use in the evaluation stage.

Accuracy was assessed in two judgement tasks:
- **Identification:** verbal descriptions were typed on cards in sets of six and the photofits were also arranged in sets of six. A new array of 24 colour faces of young adult males was constructed, containing the original six faces with an additional 18 new faces. All this was set up at various points around the university campus. Volunteer judges were sought from students, staff and visitors. Each 'judge' was randomly assigned one set of either verbal descriptions or photofits and asked to identify the target for each description/ photofit from the array of 24.

- **Sorting task:** two further groups of 16 judges (eight male and eight female) were recruited from a student subject panel. In the first group, each judge was given a pack containing the 36 verbal descriptions together with the original six photographs. Their task was to sort the descriptions into six groups of six corresponding with the photographs. The same procedure was followed by judges in the second group for the photofits. The score was the number of times each description/photofit was correctly 'sorted'.

Findings and conclusion: Analysis of both the identification and the sorting tasks suggest a marked superiority for verbal descriptions over photofit constructions. This has obvious implications for police procedure, as it suggests that recording a detailed description of the person should be given priority over the creation of a photofit image.

'Photofit constructions versus verbal descriptions of faces', *Journal of Applied Psychology* **66**, pp. 358–63

Item 4   Interviewing suspects: detecting lies

A. Vrij and S. Mann (2001): the ability of police officers to detect deception

Aim: To examine the ability of police officers to detect deception.

Sample: Fifty-two uniformed police officers from the Netherlands: 28 male and 28 female, having a mean age of 31 and a mean length of service of 9 years. The majority were tested while attending a lecture at a Dutch police school on interviewing suspects, and the remainder were tested at local police stations.

Method: The researchers had collected eight short clips from videotaped press conferences, where people were asking the general public for help in finding their relatives or the murderers of their relatives. Five of the clips were of people who had later been convicted of the crime and three clips were assumed to contain no deception. These were used as 'filler' items and are not included in the analysis. The officers had to watch each clip and then indicate:

- whether they thought the person was lying (yes/no)
- how confident they were with their decision (1–7 scale)
- whether they could understand what the person was saying (clips were in English) (yes/no)
- any behavioural cues that prompted their decisions

Findings: Three officers were right 80% of the time, 25 were right 60% of the time, 20 were right 40% of the time, three were right 20% of the time and one officer was wrong on every occasion. By chance, you would expect a score of 50%, and the authors claim that this means that those scoring 40% and 60% are therefore scoring at the chance level.

This means that 49 of the 52 officers do no better than would have been expected by simply guessing.

Age, length of service, level of experience in interviewing suspects and confidence had no effect on the accuracy scores. However, there was a correlation between level of experience in interviewing suspects and being confident in detecting deception (but not being any more accurate). Finally, men were better at detecting deception than women.

Conclusion: Detecting deception is a difficult task at which even police officers are not very good.

'Who killed my relative? Police officers' ability to detect real life high stake lies', *Psychology, Crime and Law* **7**, pp. 119–32

Item 5   Interviewing suspects: interrogation techniques

The purpose of an interrogation is to extract a confession from a suspect. Many police forces use interrogation manuals written by experienced interrogators. Interrogation methods involve:

- deception
- manipulation
- pressure
- persuasion

The most widely accepted manual for interrogation was written by **Inbau et al. (1986).** Although it is American, many of its techniques are used in the UK by both the police and the military. The interrogation procedure follows nine stages:

Step	Process
1 Direct positive confrontation	The suspect is told directly that he or she is considered to have committed the offence.
2 Theme development	The interrogator suggests to the suspect a possible account of the crime, which minimises his or her involvement or culpability. The aim is to show sympathy and understanding.
3 Handling denials	The suspect is not allowed to repeatedly deny the offence. The interrogator interrupts denials to prevent the suspect gaining a psychological advantage.
4 Overcoming objections	The interrogator does not acknowledge reasons for the suspect's innocence. Once the suspect realises that objections get him or her nowhere, he or she stops making them.
5 Procurement and retention of suspect's attention	In order to avoid withdrawal on the suspect's part, the interrogator maintains physical proximity, good eye contact and uses the suspect's first name.
6 Handling suspect's passive mood	A continuation of step 4, in which the interrogator tries to facilitate a remorseful mood in the suspect, for example by focusing on the victim's distress.

Step	Process
7 Presenting an alternative question	The suspect is presented with two accounts of the crime. Both are incriminating but one allows the suspect to explain why he or she committed the crime. Inbau et al. believe that this alternative is more attractive to the suspect.
8 Having suspect relate details of offence orally	Having accepted one of the accounts offered in step 7, the suspect gives an oral confession.
9 Converting oral into written confession.	The oral confession is put down in writing in order to overcome a possible retraction by the suspect later.

Softley (1980) observed 218 interviews with suspects conducted by English police forces to see whether the officers used any kind of persuasive tactic. Of the 218 interviews, 48% of suspects made a full confession and 13% made damaging and self-incriminating admissions. Persuasive techniques were used in 60% of interviews. The most common technique (in 22% of interviews) involved pointing out inconsistencies in the suspect's statement. Other techniques included telling the suspect that there was compelling evidence against him or her (13% of interviews) and hinting that further evidence was available (15% of interviews). However, these techniques can cause problems if the plaintiff suggests he or she was coerced into giving a false confession.

Pearse and Gudjonsson (1999)

The researchers analysed interview recordings from 18 serious crimes (ten resulting in a conviction) and found that the police tend to use six tactics in interrogations:

1 Intimidation — emphasising the experience of the police officer
2 Robust challenge — disputing the suspect's account and accusing him or her of lying
3 Manipulation — minimising the seriousness of the offence and the suspect's degree of responsibility
4 Questioning style, for example leading questions
5 Appeal — to the suspect's good character and reassuring him or her
6 Soft challenge — introducing the suspect's version of events and speaking quietly

They found that 1 and 2 were the most frequently used tactics, and they increased throughout the interview until the suspect confessed — but the police used them carefully, balancing up the likelihood that the evidence would be found inadmissible in court.

Item 6   Interviewing suspects: false confessions

R. Horselenberg, H. Merckelbach and S. Josephs (2003): individual differences and false confessions

Aim: Kassin and Kiechel (1996) falsely accused students of causing a computer crash and found that 69% of them were willing to sign a false confession, 28% of them internalised the guilt and 9% confabulated detail to support their false beliefs. Kassin and Kiechel claim that their study demonstrates how easy it is to elicit false confessions. However,

Horselenberg et al. point out that there were no negative consequences to signing this false confession and so this study lacks ecological validity. Their study is a replication of Kassin and Kiechel with the addition of negative financial consequences for falsely confessing. They also examine whether personality differences are associated with false confessions.

Sample: Thirty-four female undergraduate students with a mean age of 18.6 years were told that they were participating in a study to evaluate a new type of keyboard configuration. They were paid for their participation.

Method: Participants were asked to type characters as they appeared on a computer screen. They were told not to touch the shift key, as this would cause the computer to crash and lose all the data. Part-way through the test, the computer was made to crash and the experimenter accused the participant of touching the shift key, saying that she had seen it 'with her own eyes' (false incriminating evidence). Then the experimenter asked participants to sign a hand-written confession stating that the data was lost because the participant hit the shift key and would therefore forfeit 80% of the promised fee (negative consequence).

Findings

- 27 of the 34 students signed the confession
- 14 internalised the guilt
- 19 confabulated details

Conclusions: These results show how easy it is to elicit a false confession from someone. Individual differences as tested for with the psychometric tests did not appear to have any effect on false confessions. This suggests that false confessions are more likely to be a result of situation than personality.

'Individual differences and false confessions: a conceptual replication of Kassin and Kiechel (1996)', *Psychology, Crime and Law* **9**, pp. 1–8

Item 7   Creating an offender profile: a case study

A woman living in the USA was raped and reported the offence to the local police department. The investigating officer realised that the circumstances of the offence were similar to six previous rapes in the area and that the attacks may well have all been carried out by the same person.

The police were unable to identify a suspect, so the case files were then sent to the FBI's Behavioural Science Unit and a psychological profile constructed. This investigation concluded that the same person had committed all seven crimes. The suspect was predicted to be a white male, probably in his late twenties or early thirties, most likely to be divorced or separated and to have a job as a casual labourer or similar. It was also hypothesised that he would have had a high-school education and live in the immediate area of the offences, have a poor self-image, and have previous convictions for minor sexual offences. The FBI unit also predicted that the police in the area might have stopped the person previously, as he would probably have been out on the streets in the early hours of the morning.

Consequently, the police narrowed down their list of suspects to some 40 local males who met the age profile. Using other information provided, they then focused their investigation on one particular individual. This person was soon arrested and was subsequently convicted of all the offences.

R. Ault and J. Reese (1980) 'Profiling: a psychological assessment of crime', *FBI Law Enforcement Bulletin* 1–4

Item 8   The US (top-down) approach to offender profiling

The approach adopted by the Federal Bureau of Investigation (FBI) was two pronged. First, it conducted in-depth interviews on 36 sexually oriented murders, including those by Ted Bundy and Charles Manson. Then it collected detailed information from the Bureau's Behavioural Science Unit, which is experienced in the area of sexual crime and homicide. This information was combined with detailed examination of the crime scene, the nature of the attacks, forensic evidence and any information relating to the victim, to develop models that would result in a profile of the offender.

On the basis of this, the FBI developed a classification system for several serious crimes, including murder and rape. Criminals were classified into either 'organised' or 'disorganised' — the two types demonstrating different characteristics. This is described as profiling 'crime scene analysis'.

Having established a system, details on what should happen after a serious crime were developed as follows:
- **Stage 1 data assimilation:** collection of as much information as possible, from as many sources as possible, for example photographs and autopsy reports
- **Stage 2 crime classification:** categorisation of the crime (organised or disorganised)
- **Stage 3 crime reconstruction:** development of a hypothesis about the behaviour of victims and *modus operandi* of the criminal
- **Stage 4 profile generation:** collection of details of possible physical appearance and demographic characteristics (for example age and race), habits and personality

This type of profiling is best when investigators have important details about the suspect, such as those derived from cases of rape, arson and cult killings that involve odd or extreme practices such as sadistic torture or dissection of the body. Ordinary murder and assault do not lend themselves to profiling, as the crime scene does not yield sufficient information.

Item 9   The UK (bottom-up) approach to offender profiling

Started in the UK by David Canter, the British approach is more scientific than the FBI's, as it is based on psychological theories and methodology. It attempts to formulate psychological theories that will show how and why variations in criminal behaviour occur.

Central to the UK approach is the need to demonstrate consistencies *within* the action of offenders and identify differences *between* them.

Canter (1989) has outlined several aspects of criminal behaviour that may provide clues to other aspects of the criminal's everyday life. They include:

- **Interpersonal coherence:** the degree of violence and control varies widely between offenders, although each offender tends to be consistent in his or her treatment of the victim. These patterns of behaviour may reflect the way the criminal treats other people in everyday non-criminal life. The type of victim he or she chooses may be significant. He or she may have a grudge, for example Ted Bundy killed more than 30 students when he was a student. Therefore, the type of victim may indicate something about the assailant.
- **Significance of time and place:** Canter introduces the concept of **mental maps** in interpreting the geographical pattern of offending. Geographical profiling takes into account an individual's spatial behaviour and predicts the offender's residence based on the location of crimes, such as the sites where victims' bodies are dumped and abduction sites etc.
- **Forensic awareness:** if police have previously questioned a criminal for something similar, they need to check police records carefully. Also, systematic attempts to destroy evidence might suggest that the person has previous convictions.

Item 10   Evaluation of the two approaches to offender profiling

Boon and Davies (1992) refer to the UK approach as 'bottom-up', where you start with all the available evidence and then look for links and associations between them. The American approach is top-down, as you try to place the crime into the classification system, i.e. organised or disorganised.

Rarely does profiling provide the specific identity of the offender, and this is not its purpose. The aim is to narrow the field of the investigation and suggest the type of person who committed the crime. The profile report will try to establish the gender, approximate age, marital status, educational level and details of possible occupation of the offender. There may be suggestions of whether this person has a previous police record and if another offence is likely. Offender profiling is only appropriate for a small number of specific types of crime, for example sadistic torture in sexual assaults, lust and mutilation in murder, rape or paedophilia.

Copson (1995): is offender profiling useful?
Aim: To find out whether offender profiling improves the effectiveness of experienced detectives — do profilers provide information that is not already available?
Method: A survey of police opinion. Questionnaires used: self-report.
Participants: Police officers who had used profilers: 81% (184) returned the completed questionnaires. Most profiled crimes were murders.

Findings: Fifty per cent of respondents felt the profiler had been useful, providing an intelligent second opinion on the crime. However, only 14% felt the profiler had helped to solve the crime. Less than 3% said that the profiler had 'identified the criminal'.

Conclusion: In the UK, there is no consistency of approach to profiling, and until there is, it is difficult to measure the effectiveness of profiling.

A. Mokros and L. J. Alison (2002): is offender profiling possible?

Aim: To test the notion that the more similar the background characteristics of offenders are, the greater the resemblance in their crime scene behaviour.

Participants: One hundred male British offenders convicted of stranger rape: 61 were assumed to be 'one-off' rapists (one victim statement in police records) and the other 39 were known to have offended more than once (more than one victim statement in police records).

Methods: Crime scene actions were assessed from victim statements. Where more than one victim statement existed (see above), the earliest and latest were used. In total, 139 victim statements were analysed using content analysis. Twenty-eight crime scene actions were coded, and these included the use of disguise, the theft of personal property, verbal violence, apologies, use of blindfold, and/or use of weapon.

Information on the offenders' background characteristics was extracted from police files and included age at time of offence, ethnicity, employment status, educational level, marital status and previous criminal record (further analysed by type).

Findings and conclusion: No correlation was found between any of the variables. In other words, rapists who offend in a similar fashion are not similar with respect to age, socio-demographic features or criminal records. The authors conclude that the suggestion of socio-demographic similarity is too simplistic and they suggest that future research should consider a framework for offender profiling that is grounded in personality psychology.

'Testing the predicted homology of crime scene actions and background characteristics in a sample of rapists', *Legal and Criminological Psychology* **7**, pp. 25–43

Questions

1 Read Items 1–3.

a Describe how to interview a witness using a cognitive interview.

b Carry out research into aspects of human memory and then explain, suggesting *two* reasons, why a cognitive interview may gain more information from a witness than a standard interview.

c Describe *one* study that suggests how witnesses should (or should not) be questioned.

(Continued overleaf)

d Outline psychological research into factors that influence accurate identification.

e Evaluate psychological research into factors that influence accurate identification.

f Assess the usefulness of psychological research into factors that influence accurate identification.

2 Read Items 4–6.

a Describe research that suggests how to interrogate a suspect to gain a confession.

(Continued overleaf)

....

....

....

....

....

....

....

....

b Assess the extent to which interrogators can recognise false confessions.

....

....

....

....

....

....

....

....

....

....

....

....

c Outline and evaluate *one* study into the ability to detect deception.

....

....

....

....

....

....

....

3 Exam practice

Read Items 1–6. Make a plan for this essay, write it out in full and hand it in to be assessed.

a Describe research into *two* different aspects of witness testimony.

b Discuss the problems faced by psychologists who research how to interview witnesses.

(Continued overleaf)

4 Read Items 7–10.

   a Describe the US approach to creating an offender profile.

   b Describe the UK approach to creating an offender profile.

c Describe *one* case study of a successful offender profile.

....

....

....

....

....

....

....

....

....

d Assess, using evidence, the validity of offender profiling as a method of identifying suspects.

....

....

....

....

....

....

....

....

....

....

....

....

....

....

....

....

....

Topic 3 Reaching a verdict

This topic focuses on how psychology can explain behaviour in the courtroom. The three sections in this topic are:

- persuading a jury
- witness appeal
- reaching a verdict

At the end of this topic, you should be able to:

- describe and evaluate psychological research into factors that influence behaviour in the courtroom and jury decision making
- discuss and apply psychological research methods, perspectives and issues when considering factors that influence behaviour in the courtroom and jury decision making

Item 1 Persuading a jury

D. C. Pennington (1982): primacy and recency effects in witness testimony

Aim: To examine whether there is a primacy effect or a recency effect in relation to witness testimony. Much previous research found recency effects, demonstrating that the later information had the most powerful effect on jury decisions. However, Pennington claimed that such research did not adequately simulate a real courtroom and he predicted that the results would be different in his simulated courtroom procedure.

Participants: The participants were 192 undergraduate students (96 male and 96 female): all were eligible for jury service in the UK and any that were not were excluded from this study.

Method: A simulated courtroom procedure. This is an experimental design with independent measures. Some participants heard witnesses give 'guilty' testimonies first, and others heard witnesses give 'innocent' testimonies first. Overall, each participant was exposed to exactly the same material but in different orders.

Findings: The group that heard the guilty witnesses first produced more guilty verdicts than the other group. They were also more confident in their judgements.

Conclusion: This suggests strong primacy effects in courtroom decision making — that the evidence heard first will have the greatest persuasive effect.

'Witnesses and their testimony: effects of ordering on juror verdicts', *Journal of Applied Social Psychology* **12** (4), pp. 318–33

D. Broeder (1959): inadmissible information

Aim: To examine the effect of information being ruled inadmissible by a judge, and whether, for at least some jury members, being told to disregard information makes it even more important.

Participants: The individuals who participated were actually on jury service at the time and agreed to serve on 'experimental (mock) juries' formed by the researchers.

Method: The mock juries listened to tapes of evidence from previous trials and were asked to deliberate as if they were hearing the case. In one part of this research, 30 mock juries listened to the case of a woman who was injured by a car driven by a careless male driver.

Findings: When the driver said that he had insurance, the jurors awarded the victim an average of $4,000 more than when he said he had no insurance ($37,000 versus $33,000). This suggests that juries make larger awards to victims if an insurance company will have to pay.

The second finding is more interesting. If the driver said he was insured and the judge ruled that evidence inadmissible (directing the jury to disregard it), the average award to the victim increased to $46,000.

In other words, when juries learned that the driver was insured, they increased the damage payment by $4,000. When they were told they must officially disregard this information, they used it even more, increasing the damage payment by $13,000. This research is supported by other psychological studies, which demonstrate that banned information acquires greater salience (meaningfulness).

'The University of Chicago jury project', *Nebraska Law Review* **38**, pp. 744–60

Item 2 Witness appeal

J. E. Stewart (1985): appearance and punishment

Aim: To look for a correlation between the attractiveness of a defendant and the severity of the punishment awarded. The authors predicted a negative correlation: that is, as the attractiveness of defendants increases, the severity of punishment will decrease.

Participants: Sixty criminal trials were observed in Pennsylvania, USA. The defendants were a range of ages: 56 were male and only four were female. 27 were black, three were Hispanic and 30 were white. Eight observers were used (all white), and each was given a standard rating form (see below). Each trial was observed by at least two observers.

Method: Observers rated the defendants on a range of scales. These included physical attractiveness, neatness, cleanliness and quality of dress. These four items were combined to produce an attractiveness index. Several other ratings were also used, the most important of these being posture.

Findings: No significant correlation was found between race and the attractiveness index, and the inter-rater reliability for observer ratings was high (.78). However, the attractiveness index was negatively correlated with punitiveness — that is, the less attractive the defendants were judged to be, the more severe their punishment was. The fifth item, posture, also showed this negative correlation.

'The attraction–leniency effect in the courtroom', *The Journal of Social Psychology*, **125** (3), pp. 373–78

D. F. Ross et al. (1994): protective shields and videotape

Aim: To examine the effects on conviction rates if children give evidence in sexual abuse cases in court or with a protective shield or via videotape.

Participants: The participants were 300 students: 150 male and 150 female. The majority were white and middle class.

Method: Simulation of a sexual abuse trial. This was based on actual court transcripts and videotaped in a real courtroom using legal professionals. The video lasted 2 hours.

The independent variable was the way in which the child (a 10-year-old girl) gave her evidence. In condition 1, she gave her evidence in court directly confronting the defendant. In condition 2, she gave her evidence in the courtroom but with a protective shield. In condition 3, she gave evidence on video.

- In the first study, the participants watched the whole video and were then asked to judge the guilt of the defendant.
- In the second study, the same procedure was followed with a new sample of 300 students. However, the video was stopped immediately after the child gave her evidence and the participants were asked to make their judgement at this point.

Findings (first study): The type of testimony had no effect on conviction rates, although there was a tendency for females to return more guilty verdicts than males.

Type of testimony	% guilty verdicts	% not guilty verdicts
Open court	51	49
Protective shield	46	54
Video	49	51

Findings (second study): When evidence was given in open court, more convictions were returned than in either the protective shield or the video conditions. However, it is the effect on the final decision that is crucial, and this study demonstrates that the use of video or protective shields does not significantly reduce the likelihood of a conviction.

Conclusion: It does not appear to reduce the effectiveness of testimony if a child is not present in court to give evidence.

'The impact of protective shields and videotape testimony on conviction rates in a simulated trial of child sexual abuse', *Law and Human Behaviour* **18** (5), pp. 553–56

Loftus (1974): the importance of eyewitness evidence in the minds of jurors

Procedure: Loftus presented 150 mock jurors with a scenario about a robbery and murder in a local store. The participants were told:

- that the robber ran into the apartment block where the accused person (defendant) lived
- that money was found in the defendant's room
- that tests revealed there was a slight chance the defendant had fired a gun on the day of the robbery/murder

There were three experimental conditions:

- Condition 1: an eyewitness said he saw a man leaving the store. In this condition, 72% of mock jurors found the defendant guilty.
- Condition 2: there was no eyewitness evidence and only 18% of mock jurors found the defendant guilty.
- Condition 3: there was an eyewitness, but his evidence was discredited because it was established that he was short-sighted, not wearing his glasses at the time of the offence, and could not have seen the robber's face from where he was standing. In this condition, 68% of mock jurors found the defendant guilty.

Conclusion: Producing an eyewitness has a powerful influence on jury decision making.

Item 3 Reaching a verdict

The story model of juror decision making

Lawyers can either present evidence in chronological order (story order) or in the way they think will influence the jury best (witness order), for example with the most persuasive evidence first. Evidence suggests that members of the jury construct a story in order to make sense of the evidence presented.

Pennington and Hastie (1990) requested that mock jurors carried out their deliberations out loud. They conducted many studies that provided substantial empirical evidence for the story model. They suggest that jurors construct their story in three stages:

- **Stage 1 construction of the story:** jurors consider the actual evidence and use their knowledge of the world to interpret evidence and come to conclusions about what happened. Jurors have three types of information:
  - information acquired during trial
  - knowledge about events that are similar, for example a similar crime committed in jurors' community
  - expectations, based on experience, about what makes a complete story
- **Stage 2 learning verdict definitions:** instead of just deciding guilty or not guilty, jurors like to decide how guilty. They have to learn the different categories available for the judge to sentence, such as murder or manslaughter etc. (in the USA: first-degree murder/second-degree murder/manslaughter)
- **Stage 3 making a decision:** jurors have to match the story with the categories available.

While the story model proposes three stages of decision making, because each juror has different experiences and beliefs, each one may respond to the same situation or offence in an entirely different way.

Item 4 Factors that might affect the story interpretation

Attribution theory and biases in jurors and witnesses

Heider (1958) said that it is possible to explain behaviour as caused by situational or dispositional factors: dispositional attributions are based on an individual's personality, whereas situational attributions suggest that the cause is beyond a person's control. Research suggests that we make internal or dispositional attributions ('That is a nasty person') about others in order to explain their behaviour, whereas we make situational attributions about ourselves ('It was not my fault — it was due to the situation I was in').

The fundamental attribution error (FAE) (Ross 1977)

Most people explain others' behaviour by overestimating the role of personal factors and underestimating the impact of the situation. For example, a person who has an accident while driving could be reckless (dispositional), or driving too fast to get to the hospital because his wife has been injured (situational).

Just-world hypothesis

Lerner (1980) said that people need to believe the world is a just place, where 'bad things do not happen to good people'. However, where you have two opposing beliefs or theories, these cause psychological discomfort (dissonance) because they contradict each other.

Therefore, to cope with these feelings of discomfort, we have to try to find an excuse or justification for the times when people do not behave in a just way. In jury decision making, jurors can:

- blame the victims for their misfortune — the victim of burglary did not lock up securely
- vilify the character of the victims and suggest they deserve their fate, for example battered wives provoke their husbands, rape victims should not be drunk
- help victims or compensate them

One worrying aspect of the effect of the just-world hypothesis is attitudes to rape victims, for example 'She must have egged him on'. **Bell et al.** (1994) used a simulated jury to decide on four cases of two rapes by strangers and two 'date rapes'. Both males and females placed considerably more responsibility on the victim in the date rapes.

Decision making biased by the 'outcome' of behaviour

Walster (1966) found that adults judge on the basis of responsibility. People were asked to judge the amount of responsibility held by a car owner whose car had rolled down the hill when the brake cable broke because it had rusted. The car either injured someone or was deflected and did no damage. Subjects were asked to judge whether the car owner was:

- not responsible
- slightly responsible
- somewhat responsible
- very responsible

Participants attributed more responsibility to the owner when someone was hurt. However, this study was criticised, because 'responsible' might mean different things to different people.

Item 5   Majority and minority influence in jury decision making (social influence)

Social influence is the way that a person or group of people can affect the attitudes and behaviour of another individual.

Majority influence (conformity) is the process that takes place when an individual's attitudes or behaviour is affected by the views of the dominant group. This may be because of normative social influence (the effect of social norms) but can also occur because of informational social influence, when the minority yields to group pressure because it thinks that the majority has more knowledge or information.

Normative social influence occurs when an individual agrees with the opinions of a group of people because he or she wishes to be accepted by them. The influenced individual may not change his or her private belief.

Informational social influence occurs when a question asked does not have an obviously correct answer. When this happens, people look to others for information and may agree with the majority view. Informational social influence involves the process of compliance.

Types of conformity

Compliance is when a person conforms to the majority opinion but does not really agree with it. This is evidenced because if the group pressure is removed, the conformity will cease. Compliance is thought to occur because an individual wishes to be accepted by the majority group.

Identification is another type of conformity that occurs when the person conforms to the behaviour expected by the majority (such as obeying school rules about uniform) but without enthusiasm. Identification is thought to occur because an individual wishes to belong to a group.

Internalisation occurs when an individual conforms because he or she believes that a group norm for behaviour or a group attitude is 'right'. If group pressure is removed, this conformity will continue.

Minority influence is the process that takes place when a consistent minority changes the attitudes and or behaviour of an individual. Social psychologists propose that it is the consistency of the minority that is important, since it demonstrates a firm alternative view to that of the majority. Minority influence leads to a change in attitudes and involves the process of conversion.

Item 6   Research into conformity

Asch (1956): conformity as the result of normative social influence

Aim: To discover how much the majority influences the decisions of individuals during an unambiguous task.

Procedures: In a laboratory experiment with a repeated measures design, groups of seven or eight male students were shown a stimulus line (S) and then three other lines (A, B and C). There was only one 'real' participant in each group. The others were confederates who were helping the experimenter. All the participants were asked to say out loud which line (A, B or C) matched the stimulus line. The real participant always answered last or last but one. Each participant completed 18 trials, and in 12 of the trials (the critical trials), the confederates had been primed to all give the same wrong answer.

Findings: In the control trials, real participants gave 0.7% incorrect answers. In the critical trials, real participants gave 37% incorrect answers, which conformed to the majority answer. Seventy-five per cent of the real participants conformed at least once. After the experiment, the real participants were asked why they answered as they had, and some said that they did not really believe their answer but they had not wanted to look different.

Conclusion: Normative social influence had taken place: the real participants agreed with the opinion of the group because they wished to be accepted by it. This demonstrated that participants gave wrong answers because of compliance rather than from conversion.

Moscovici et al. (1969): a study of minority influence

Aim: To find out whether consistency in the minority is an important factor in minority influence.

Procedures: In a laboratory experiment, female student participants were randomly allocated to either a consistent, inconsistent or control condition. There were six participants in each condition — four naive participants (who formed the majority) and two confederates (the minority). In the control condition there were no confederates. All participants were tested for colour blindness. Participants were asked to name the colour of 36 slides, all of which were blue but which varied in brightness.

- In the consistent condition, the confederates named all 36 slides as green.
- In the inconsistent condition, the confederates named 24 of the slides as green and 12 slides as blue.

Minority influence was measured by the percentage of naive participants' answers that called the blue slides green (followed the minority influence).

Findings: In the consistent condition, 8.42% of the participants' answers were green and 32% gave the incorrect answer at least once. In the inconsistent condition, 1.25% of the participants' answers were green. In the control condition, only 0.25% of the participants' answers were green. The consistent condition showed the greatest conformity to minority influence.

Conclusions: A minority can influence individuals' behaviour and beliefs, and this influence is more likely when the minority is consistent. Therefore, in jury trials a consistent minority may influence the majority.

Characteristics of influential minorities

Moscovici (1985) suggested five characteristics of the behaviour of influential minorities:

- They are consistent, demonstrating certainty, and they draw attention to their views.
- They enter into discussion and avoid being too dogmatic.
- They take action in support of their principles (for example take part in protest marches).
- They make sacrifices to maintain their views.
- They are similar, in terms of age, class and gender, to the population they are trying to influence.

Questions

1 Read Item 1.

a Outline research evidence into techniques that can be used to persuade a jury.

b Assess the problems faced by psychologists who research jury persuasion.

(Continued overleaf)

....

....

....

....

....

....

....

....

....

....

....

2 Read Item 2.

a Describe research into how the 'appeal' of the witness might affect jury decision making.

....

....

....

....

....

....

....

....

....

....

....

b Evaluate research into how the 'appeal' of the witness might affect jury decision making.

....

....

c Assess the usefulness of research into how the 'appeal' of the witness might affect jury decision making.

3 Read Items 3 and 4.

a Describe *one* theory (model) as to how jurors make their decisions.

b Outline and explain *two* cognitive factors that may bias jury decision making.

....

....

....

....

....

....

....

....

....

4 Read Items 5–7.

a Explain how social influence may affect jury decision making.

....

....

....

....

....

....

....

....

....

....

....

....

....

b Describe *one* study of majority influence and explain how this may affect how a jury reaches a verdict.

c In relation to jury decision making, evaluate research into majority and minority influence.

5 Exam practice

Read Items 1–7. Make a plan for this essay, write it out in full, and hand it in to be assessed.

a Describe psychological research into jury decision making.

b Discuss the usefulness of research into behaviour in the courtroom.

Topic 4 After a guilty verdict

The three sections this topic cover:
- imprisonment
- alternatives to imprisonment
- treatment programmes

At the end of this topic, you should be able to:
- describe and evaluate psychological research into how psychology can inform the penal system
- discuss and apply psychological research methods, perspectives and issues when considering psychological research applied to the penal system

Item 1 Imprisonment

D. P. Farrington, J. Ditchfield, P. Howard and D. Jolliffe (2002): intensive regimes and young offenders

Aim: To test the impact of demanding, highly structured regimes on reconviction rates 2 years after release.

Sample: Young offenders: male, aged between 18 and 21, with approximately 6 months' sentence left to serve. They were considered suitable for open prison (no previous escape or sex offences) and mentally and physically able to cope with the regime.

Method: Two institutions were studied. Both were styled on US 'boot camp' regimes:
- Thorn Cross High Intensity Training Centre (opened July 1996). This centre offers a highly structured 25-week, 16-hours-a-day programme of activities including military drilling.
- Colchester Young Offender Institution (opened in February 1997). This has a 26-week programme based on the military regime and ethos at the Military Corrective Training Centre at Colchester.

The expected reconviction rates were calculated and these were compared with actual reconviction rates 2 years after release. Reconviction rates were also compared with a control group of young offenders in 'standard regime' institutions.

Findings

Thorn Cross: although there were no significant differences in the proportion of offenders who were reconvicted when comparing the Thorn Cross experimental group and the control group, the experimental group took longer to re-offend and committed significantly fewer crimes. The authors conclude that the cost of the regime was more than recouped by the savings made by the smaller number of crimes committed, and estimate that approximately £5 was saved for every £1 spent on the regime.

Colchester: although the Colchester experimental group committed slightly fewer crimes than a control group, their crimes were more costly, and the authors estimate that this regime was not cost effective. However, the Colchester group had significantly more positive attitudes towards staff and other inmates and were more hopeful about the future.

Conclusion: The authors conclude that the success of the Thorn Cross regime in reducing reconviction rates was probably due to the education, employment, mentoring and 'through-care' components rather than to the drilling and physical training components of the Colchester regime, which suggests physical activities were not successful.

'Two intensive regimes for young offenders: a follow up evaluation', Home Office Research, Development and Statistics Directorate Research Findings No. 163

Item 2   Risk factors associated with self-harm or suicide in UK prisoners

The Youth Justice Board for England and Wales is an executive non-departmental public body employed to:
- advise the home secretary on the operation of the youth justice system, how to prevent offending by children and young people, and the content of national standards for youth justice services
- monitor the operation and performance of the youth justice system

www.publications.parliament.uk/pa/cm200405/cmselect/cmdfence/63/63we120.htm

Deliberate self-harm within prison

Self-harm is a significant issue for adolescents within prison. **Liebling (1995)** examined factors associated with self-harm in young prisoners. In these studies, it was noted that all the prisoners had backgrounds with multiple disadvantages. Suicide attempters were more likely to report multiple family breakdown, frequent violence leading to hospitalisation, local authority placement as a result of family breakdown, truancy as a result of bullying, experiences of sexual abuse and previous episodes of self-harm. The suicide attempters found prison life more difficult in most respects. Liebling called this group of young people 'poor copers'.

Suicide within prison

Within prison, 10% of suicides occur within the first 24 hours of imprisonment, 40% within the first month and 80% within the first year. Studies on prison suicide have highlighted the importance of both individual and institutional factors. In studies of completed suicides in England and Wales **(Dooley 1990; HM Chief Inspector of Prisons 1999)**, risk factors identified included mental illness, a history of psychiatric contact (40%), a history of single or multiple substance misuse (30–70%), a history of self-harm (50%), loss of social contact and relationship difficulties, victimisation by other inmates, and difficulties in coping with the prison regime.

Item 3   Alternatives to imprisonment

D. Sugg, L. Moore and P. Howard (2001): electronic monitoring curfew orders

Aim: To examine the effectiveness of electronic monitoring curfew orders.

Sample: The sample consisted of 261 offenders from Norfolk, Manchester and Reading who had been given curfew orders with electronic monitoring between July 1996 and June 1997 (the second year of the 'tagging' trials). Ninety-one per cent of the sample were male, and most were in their mid to late 20s. Typical offences were theft, burglary and driving offences. The average number of previous convictions was eight.

Method: The probability of the sample being reconvicted was calculated using OGRS2. This is a Home Office algorithm that predicts the probability of an offender being reconvicted based on age, criminal history and time in youth custody. This suggested that the sample could be considered to be of medium to high risk of reconviction. The analysis suggested 67% would be reconvicted at the end of 2 years. This prediction was then compared with actual reconviction rates.

Results: Within 2 years, 72.8% (190/261) had been reconvicted, and 166 of those reconvicted were within 1 year. The researchers also compared the reconviction rates of the tagged group with a matched comparison group of offenders sentenced to community service orders (the most likely alternative had tagging not been available). There was no significant difference between these two groups; 160 of the 261 also had community service orders running in addition to the tagging. There was also no significant difference between this sub-group and the remaining 101 offenders in terms of reconviction rates.

Conclusions: The authors conclude that curfew orders have no significant effect on offending behaviour and they argue that this is because such orders do not address the real problems.

'Electronic monitoring and offending behaviour — reconviction results for the second year of trals of curfew orders', Home Office Research, *Development and Statistics Directorate Research Findings* No. 141

Item 4   Alternatives to imprisonment

Eberhardt et al. (2006): stereotypicality of black defendants and the death sentence

Aim: To investigate (in the USA) whether there was support for the hypothesis that black offenders with stereotypically black features were more likely to get the death sentence than white offenders.

Procedure: An investigation was carried out into the correlation between 'stereotypically black' features in offenders and the likelihood of being given the death sentence. An analysis of the database of death-eligible cases in Philadelphia between 1979 and 1999 was carried out: in 44 cases, a black man had killed a white victim. Photographs of these 44 offenders were shown to naive raters, who were asked to rate their facial features for stereotypical black features between 1 and 11 (11 was 'very stereotypical'). The 51 raters included 32 white people, 15 Asians and four people of other ethnicities.

Results: It was found that the most stereotypically black defenders were 57.5% more likely to receive the death penalty than the less stereotypical defendants at 24.4%. In a second study, where the victim was also black, no significant effect was found, suggesting black victims are seen as less important.

Conclusion: This suggests that black men who look 'stereotypically black' are seen as somehow more 'deathworthy'.

J.L. Eberhardt et al. (2006) 'Looking deathworthy: perceived stereotypicality of black defendants predicts capital-sentencing outcomes'

Item 5   Treatment programmes: cognitive skills training

C. Friendship, L. Blud, M. Erikson and R. Travers (2002): prisoners and CBT

Aim: To evaluate the success of cognitive behavioural treatments for prisoners.

Sample: The participants were 670 adult male offenders serving a custodial sentence of 2 years or more, who voluntarily took part in one of two cognitive skills programmes run by HM Prison Service between 1992 and 1996.

Method: Two multi-modal programmes were used, which focused on correcting faulty thinking patterns that have been linked with offending behaviour. The programmes were 'Reasoning and rehabilitation' (36 × 2-hour sessions) and 'Enhanced thinking skills' (20 × 2-hour sessions). The aims of the social skills training programme are:

- self-control (thinking before acting)
- interpersonal problem-solving skills
- social perspective taking
- critical reasoning skills
- cognitive style
- understanding the rules that govern behaviour

Reconviction rates were compared with a group of 1,801 male offenders who had not participated in any programme.

Results: The results showed a significant drop in reconviction rates. Reconviction rates after 2 years were up to 14% lower than the comparison groups. The authors concluded that based on the number of prisoners expected to complete a cognitive skills programme in 2002/03, this reduction represented almost 21,000 crimes prevented.

'An evaluation of cognitive behavioural treatment for prisoners', Home Office Research, *Development and Statistics Directorate Research Findings* No. 161

Item 6   Treatment programmes: anger management

Anger management is a therapeutic treatment programme that assumes violence is caused by anger, and that if violent individuals learn to control their anger, their violent behaviour will decrease.

Anger management programmes are based largely on cognitive-behavioural therapy techniques. Such a programme has been devised for use in prisons, its main focus being to try to reduce the amount of violence, but also with the hope that improved self-control will continue once offenders are released. The aims of the National Anger Management Course for Prisoners is for course members to:

- increase their understanding of how and why they become angry
- realise the importance of monitoring their own behaviour so that they notice the first signs of becoming angry
- develop strategies for controlling their anger
- use role play to practise coping with provocation
- consider how their lives will improve if they learn to control their anger and aggression

A typical course involves around eight 2-hour sessions, spread over a couple of weeks, and the programme has been used in adult prisons and in institutions for young offenders. A study was carried out by **Ireland (2000)** in one young offenders' institution, to attempt to evaluate the effectiveness of anger management objectively, comparing the aggression levels of individuals before and after the treatment programme. Levels of aggression were measured in three ways:

- a record of the prisoner's aggressive behaviour as seen by the prison officers over a period of 1 week
- a cognitive style interview with the prisoner about his temper and aggression
- a 53-item self-report questionnaire completed by the prisoner

These measures were taken 2 weeks before the start of the course, and again 8 weeks later. Results showed an improvement on at least one measure in 92% of participants, and on two measures in 48% of participants; 8% of prisoners were worse after the treatment. The sample size was 50, and the treatment programme involved twelve 1-hour sessions, over 3 days. Ireland concluded that the programme was useful for reducing aggression in the short term.

Item 7   Ear acupuncture as treatment for substance abuse

Around 130,000 offenders flow into prisons in the UK each year, and 70,000 inmates have a substance misuse problem. This research was designed to assess the efficacy of ear acupuncture as an additional treatment for substance misuse.

After screening to ensure no substance abuse in the last 30 days, the volunteer patients were allocated to two groups: one was the treatment group, which received twice-weekly acupuncture treatments along with standard care for a 4-week period; the second control group received only standard care. Data were gathered using:

- the Background Information Questionnaire (BIQ), to gather demographic data
- the Alcohol Dependency Scale (ADS), to measure problematic alcohol use
- the Drug Abuse Screening Test (DAST), to measure severity of the drug abuse problem

The control group's health distress symptoms improved by 25%, whereas the treatment group's symptoms improved by 43%. This suggests that ear acupuncture is 18% more effective than standard care.

In the ear acupuncture group:

- worry levels reduced by 30%
- drug craving reduced by 47%
- psychological wellbeing improved by 53%
- there was a 27% increase in confidence to address drug and alcohol problems

Therefore, it can be concluded that ear acupuncture, as an addition to standard care, improves patients' health and wellbeing, improves sleep and relaxation, reduces cravings and also improves the patient's chance of tackling the problem because patients were more likely to access and participate in other support programmes.

SMART UK and M. Wheatley (2007) 'An evaluation of SMART UK auricular acupuncture with substance misusing male prisoners in maximum security prisons', SMS, Directorate of Higher Estates. Evaluated by A. Liebling and S. Maruna, Institute of Criminology, University of Cambridge

Questions

1 Read Items 1 and 2.

a Outline *one* study that looks at the effectiveness of imprisonment.

b Outline research that looks at the effect of imprisonment on young offenders.

c Evaluate the usefulness of research into imprisonment.

(Continued overleaf)

2 Read Items 3 and 4.

    a Write a synopsis of Eberhardt et al.'s research study 'Looking deathworthy', in the format: aim, procedures, findings and conclusions.

b Describe and evaluate psychological research into *one* alternative to imprisonment
(a non-custodial punishment).

....

....

....

....

....

....

....

....

....

....

....

....

....

c Assess the problems faced by psychologists who try to research the effectiveness of
offender punishments.

....

....

....

....

....

....

....

....

....

....

3 Read Items 5–7.

a Describe research into the effectiveness of offender treatment programmes.

....

....

....

....

....

....

....

....

....

....

....

....

....

....

b Evaluate the strengths and weaknesses of the research you described in **a**.

....

....

....

....

....

....

....

....

....

....

....

....

c Assess, using evidence, the effectiveness of offender treatment programmes.

....

....

....

....

....

....

....

....

....

....

....

....

....

4 Exam practice

Read Items 1–7. Make a plan for this essay, write it out in full and hand it in to be assessed.

a Describe psychological research into *two* aspects of the penal system.

b Evaluate the strengths and weaknesses of the methods used to investigate the effectiveness of punishments and treatments.

....

....

....

(Continued overleaf)